D1390286

The Rare
with the
Colourful Bottom

Published by Patterns in the Jam 2014
First edition 2014
ISBN 978 0 9930890 0 8
All text copyright © Joanne Gale 2014
All illustrations copyright © Jeffrey Mundell 2014

Printed and bound in the UK
by CPI Group (UK) Ltd, Croydon, CR0 4YY

MIX
Paper from
responsible sources
FSC® C013604

9030 00005 2276 3

In the wild there was a very shy and sad monkey. He was sad because he was different. He was the only one who had a colourful bottom.

Lots of wild animals have colourful fur, feathers or skin. But only the monkey's bottom was...

...bright and full of lots of different colours!

He had lost hope of finding someone else with a bottom like his.

Every day in the wild the animals would make fun of his bottom.

The grey elephants would throw their trunks up and laugh.

The yellow lions would roar and giggle.

4

...and chuckle so hard that his shell shook like jelly.
Even the birds who were bright green would
squawk and joke.

When the monkey climbed a tree the other monkeys cackled with laughter.

None of them had a strange multicoloured bottom.

The colourful-bottomed monkey felt alone.

One day the animals joked so much that the monkey decided to leave.

He crept out of sight, avoiding anyone he saw and making sure he hid his bottom from anyone who might see.

He hurried away.
Soon he no longer saw the plants and trees.

He saw cars and people. He heard strange noises and smelt unusual smells. The monkey found himself in a town.

In the town he saw strangely shaped buildings...

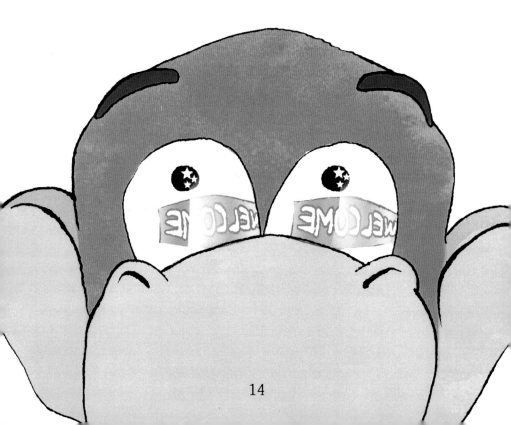

14

...and people wearing unusual clothes.

Would someone here have a bottom like his?

Down a street the monkey spotted a brown dog. He tried to hide his colourful bottom in case the dog laughed. But the dog didn't laugh. He strode past and smiled.

The monkey found a grey cat lazing on a bench. He hid his bottom. But the cat didn't make fun of him.

She told the monkey that being colourful didn't make him any better. The monkey wondered what she meant.

The monkey came across a young girl with a camera. He tried to hide his bottom, but...SNAP!... she took a photo. She had never seen an animal as bright as he was.

She gave the monkey the photo and he saw his bottom. It certainly was bright!

Was he always going to be made fun of and feel shy and sad?

The monkey sat quietly and thought.

The next day the monkey saw the same girl. She was wearing a bright red jumper and green, pink and yellow bands in her hair.

She noticed the monkey and smiled.

The next day he saw her wearing...

...purple trousers...

...orange shoes...

...and a multicoloured hat.

She took another photo and this time the monkey smiled.

She was nearly as colourful as he was.

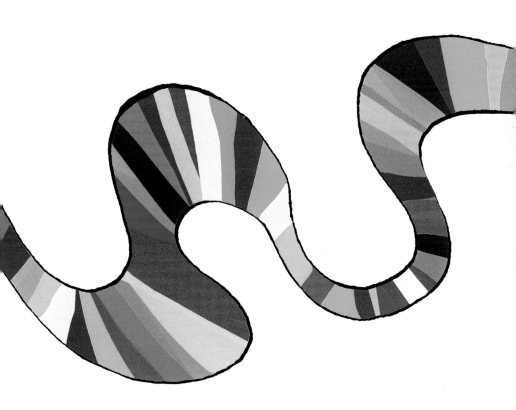

Soon the monkey saw people all over the town wearing more colourful clothes.

Everyone was bright like his bottom!

But the town was not like the wild.

The monkey missed the plants and trees. He kept the girl's photo and headed for home.

Soon he saw the grey elephants, yellow lions, brown tortoise and green birds.

34

They laughed, giggled and chuckled, but this time the monkey decided not to feel shy and sad. He held his photo tightly and smiled the largest smile he could.

The other monkeys suddenly felt very
strange for laughing.

The lions' guffaw faded and the elephants stopped joking.

The birds stared. The tortoise slowly turned, but swallowed his chuckle when he saw no one else making fun.

They all saw how splendid the monkey was now that he paid no attention to their joking.

"What counts is being yourself and liking who you are," thought the monkey and he was never shy or sad about his bright bottom again.

He is now very happy to be...

The Rare Monkey with the Colourful Bottom!

The End.